From Your Friends At **The MAILBOX**®

W9-CII-048

Busy Kids™
CIRCLE TIME

Written by:
Jan Brennan
Ann Flagg
Lisa Leonardi
Dayle Timmons

Edited by:
Ada Goren

Illustrated by:
Susan Hodnett
Rebecca Saunders

Cover designed by:
Kimberly Richard

©1998 by THE EDUCATION CENTER, INC.
All rights reserved.
ISBN #1-56234-235-5

Except as provided for herein, no part of this publication may be reproduced or transmitted in any form or by any means, electronic or mechanical, including photocopying, recording, or storing in any information storage and retrieval system or electronic on-line bulletin board, without prior written permission from The Education Center, Inc. Permission is given to the original purchaser to reproduce patterns and reproducibles for individual classroom use only and not for resale or distribution. Reproduction for an entire school or school system is prohibited. Please direct written inquiries to The Education Center, Inc., P.O. Box 9753, Greensboro, NC 27429-0753. The Education Center®, The Mailbox®, Busy Kids™, and the mailbox/post/grass logo are trademarks of The Education Center, Inc., and may be the subject of one or more federal trademark registrations. All other brand or product names are trademarks or registered trademarks of their respective companies.

Manufactured in the United States
10 9 8 7 6 5 4 3 2 1

Busy Kids™
Circle Time

Table Of Contents

Introduction

If circle-time preparations have you running in circles, then *Busy Kids™: Circle Time* is the resource for you! Turn the page to find helpful strategies and creative activities for one of the most essential segments of the preschool or kindergarten child's school day. And the activities are arranged around popular early-childhood themes you love! Each original activity has been developed to focus on early-childhood skills and concepts in inviting and playful ways. But before you invite *your* busy kids to circle time, check out the tips below.

What's the buzz on circle time?

- **"Bee" consistent.** Any time you gather your students together can be a circle time. But since young children thrive on routine, try to choose at least one regular daily circle time. You may prefer to come together first thing in the morning or to share and summarize each day at a closing circle time.

- **"Bee" comfortable.** Gather children on the carpet or around a cozy rug; then sit as close as you can so that *everyone* can see you and any materials you are using.

- **"Bee" safe.** Have children sit "crisscross applesauce" or "like a pretzel" (cross-legged) so that bottoms stay on the floor and no one steps on extended fingers or toes.

- **"Bee" prepared.** Prepare all materials in advance and have them readily available.

- **"Bee" brief.** Plan activities with your students' attention spans in mind.

- **"Bee" flexible.** If an activity isn't working, stop and go on to something else. Your children's needs and interests are more important than any lesson plan. On the other hand, extend an activity if it sparks children's interests.

- **"Bee" diverse.** Use a variety of activities and approaches to reinforce basic skills and concepts.

- **"Bee" creative.** Use humor, suspense, surprise, and any other teacher's tricks of the trade to captivate and educate your busy kids!

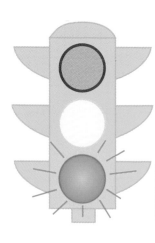

From Start To Finish

Just Sing A Little Song

Here's an itsy-bitsy tip to begin your circle time or to gain little ones' attention. Select a favorite song that has motions, such as "The Itsy-Bitsy Spider." Whisper the words of the song while doing the motions. Encourage your youngsters to join you. Then repeat the song by simply mouthing the words to the motions. All distractions will be "washed out" and all eyes will be on the teacher!

Puppet Power

Sock it to your circle time with puppet power. A puppet is always a crowd pleaser, so introduce a classroom puppet (or make one from a sock) as your circle-time mascot. Here are a few puppet pointers:

- Begin circle time with a knock on the door of the puppet's house—a covered basket or box. Ask if the puppet wants to come out and speak to the children.
- Invent a unique voice for the puppet.
- Have the puppet reward children who are displaying positive behavior with a big "sloppy" kiss.
- When you record children's thoughts or responses on chart paper, have the puppet hold the marker with which you write.

You Oughta Be In Pictures

Ready to begin circle time? Then try this picture-perfect idea. Pretend that you are a photographer preparing to take a picture with an imaginary camera. Say, "Smile for the camera." As you capture each child's attention, call out his name and pretend to snap his picture. Once everyone is looking at the camera, take a class picture. Your students will be ready to focus on circle-time activities in a snap!

Today's Headlines

Close your day on a newsworthy note by reviewing the day's events in the form of a class newspaper. Record the date on a sheet of chart paper. Then encourage youngsters to dictate sentences describing the activities of the day as you record them on the chart paper. Invite the class to echo you as you read each sentence aloud. Then place the news outside the classroom door prior to dismissal. The news will provide parents with valuable information and will enable them to ask specific questions about their child's day. The daily news is sure to get rave reviews!

Greetings

Greet your youngsters and bid them farewell each day with this personalized song. To prepare, spray-paint a three-pound coffee can. Gather an individual photograph of each child, and attach a self-adhesive magnetic strip to the back. Place the photos inside the coffee can. When circle time begins, select a photo from the can and insert that child's name into the second line of the following song. Then attach his picture to the outside of the can. Continue selecting photos and singing to each child.

Hello/Goodbye
(sung to the tune of "Polly Wolly Doodle")

Oh, you know I have a special place
I keep my [child's name] in.
I'll take [her] out
And say, "Hello!
Now let your day begin."

At the end of the day, sing the same tune to the words below as you return each child's photo to the can.

Oh, you know I have a special place
I keep my [child's name] in.
I'll tuck [her] in
And say, "Good-bye!
Until we meet again."

Today's Headlines
October 4

We made pumpkin muffins.
We read a story about a girl
and her teddy bear.
We played Duck, Duck, Goose
at the playground.

BUNNIES AND BASKETS

BUNNY WAND

Hop to it and create this adorable bunny wand! It's perfect to use as a pointer for reading songs, poems, and charts. Or wave it over your youngsters' heads and magically turn them into quiet little bunnies before you begin your circle time. Or pass it around during sharing time to indicate whose turn it is to talk.

To make a bunny wand, spray-paint a wooden spoon white. Cut bunny ears from white tagboard; then rub a cotton swab in powdered blush and add a bit of pink to the inside of the ears. Also from white tagboard, cut two bunny teeth. Then hot-glue the ears, teeth, two wiggle eyes, and a pink pom-pom nose onto the spoon as shown. If desired, tie a length of ribbon into a large bow and glue it to the spoon as a bow tie or a fancy hair bow.

COLORFUL EGGS

Send your little bunnies hoppin' on their way to stronger color-recognition skills with this colorful song. To prepare, collect enough colored plastic eggs for each child to have at least one. Have students sit in a circle; then place a basket in the center. Distribute the eggs and have each student identify the color of her egg. Then teach the song below. If a child has an egg that corresponds to the color in the song, have her hop to the basket and put her egg in. Continue with other colors until all your eggs are in one basket!

EGGS IN MY BASKET

(sung to the tune of "Skip To My Lou")

[Pink, pink, pink] little eggs.
[Pink, pink, pink] little eggs.
[Pink, pink, pink] little eggs.
[Pink] eggs in my basket.

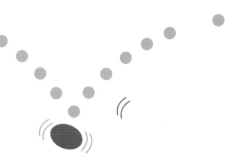

BUNCHES OF BUNNIES

Get things hoppin' with this silly countdown rhyme. Have each child use his ten fingers to represent the ten little bunnies. Instruct each youngster to fold down one finger with each bunny that hops out of the basket.

(sung to the tune of "There Were Ten In The Bed")

Ten bunnies in the basket and the little one said,
Hop over! Hop over!
So they all hopped over,
And one hopped out.

(Continue counting down nine bunnies…eight bunnies…until you get to one bunny.)

One bunny in the basket and he sang out,

(sung to the tune of "He's Got The Whole World In His Hands")

"I've got the whole basket to myself.
I've got the whole basket to myself.
I've got the whole basket to myself.
I've got the whole basket to myself. Yippee!"

Ten bunnies in the basket and the little one said...

A-TISKET, A-TASKET, A NEW LEARNING BASKET

This alphabet activity is "eggs-actly" what you want to reinforce letter identification and sounds. Place a class supply of plastic eggs in a basket. Write each letter of the alphabet on an individual slip of paper; then put one letter inside each egg. (Or use magnetic or wooden alphabet letters instead.) Select one child to be the bunny; then have him hop about, distributing an egg to each child. Ask each youngster to open his egg, identify his letter, and name a word that begins with that letter sound. If desired, modify the activity to have children name a word with the same ending sound, name an object in the room that begins with the same sound, or find a matching alphabet letter in the print around the room. It's a basket of alphabet fun!

WHAT'S IN A NAME?

Combine each little one's name with this hip-hop chant that reinforces the sound of *H*. Substitute an *H* for the initial consonant in each child's name. If a child's name begins with an *H* (like Hannah), put an additional *H* at the beginning *(H-Hannah)*. Pause at the end of the last line to allow the child to shout out his name. Youngsters will find this name game h-hilarious!

Hippity, hoppity,
Hippity [H-ared].
Hippity, hoppity,
[His] name is …[Jared]!

Christmas

Jingle bells, jingle bells...

The Sounds Of Christmas

Ring in the holiday with a jingling review of Christmas sounds. To prepare, put several jingle bells inside a clean, empty potato-chip canister. Secure the lid; then wrap the canister with some holiday paper. Have the children sit in a circle; then roll the canister to one student as you recite the following verse:

Jingle bells, jingle bells, roll around.
Can you name a Christmas sound?

Ask the child who receives the canister to name a sound associated with Christmas, such as sleigh bells ringing, a fireplace crackling, or Santa saying, "Ho, ho, ho." Then have him roll the canister to someone else. The recipient repeats the sound named by the previous child, then names a Christmas sound of his own. Continue until there are no more sounds to go around!

Reindeer!

The Sights Of Christmas

Your youngsters will gain a little "insight" into vocabulary with this holiday idea. Prepare a set of holiday cards by cutting pictures from old Christmas cards featuring holiday designs such as ornaments, poinsettias, or Christmas trees. If desired, include symbols associated with multicultural holidays such as Hanukkah and Kwanzaa. Mount each picture on an index card; then distribute one card to each child. Provide clues to describe one of the holiday pictures. Encourage the child whose picture matches the description to hold up his card for all to see. Name—or have the child name—the picture on his card. Then continue to describe the sights of the season.

Mmm, chocolate!

The Touch Of Christmas

Christmas is full of surprises, and so is a game of Santa's Secret Sack. In advance select a few Christmas-related items of different shapes, such as a wrapped candy cane, a small wreath and a non-breakable ornament. Put one of the items in a large pillowcase (without youngsters seeing the item). Then don a Santa hat and recite the following poem. Once everyone has had a turn to reach into the bag, ask the class to identify the contents of the pillowcase. Continue the game with the remaining items.

What's inside Santa's sack?
Reach right in and touch.
Can you tell what it might be?
Do you have a hunch?

The Smells Of Christmas

Have your youngsters take a whiff of this "scent-sational" activity to heighten the senses. In advance place enough Hershey's® Kisses® or mini candy canes for each child inside a box; then wrap the box in holiday paper. Carefully make several small slits in the box to allow the fragrance to filter through. Have your youngsters sit in a circle; then pass the box to a child. Ask him to smell it, think about what might be inside, and then pass it to the next child. After everyone has had a chance to smell the box, ask children to guess the contents. Record their responses; then open the box to see if anyone guessed correctly.

The Shapes Of Christmas

Watch math concepts shape up with a holiday flannelboard. Cut from felt a large green triangle, a yellow star, a brown rectangle, small colorful circles and ovals, and various sizes of squares and rectangles. Distribute the felt cutouts randomly. Have the children identify the various felt shapes; then challenge them to work together to make a Christmas picture using all of the felt cutouts. You may be surprised by what takes shape!

CIRCUS

Nuts About Elephants

Reinforce counting skills as your little animal trainers prepare to feed some hungry elephants. In advance put ten unshelled peanuts in a zippered plastic bag for every two students in your group. Divide your group into pairs. Designate one child in each pair as the elephant, and give him a paper cup. Designate the other child as the trainer and give her the bag of peanuts. After reciting the chant below, ask one elephant to call out a number. Then have each trainer count that number of peanuts from her bag into her elephant's cup. Do a quick check of the cups and assist with the counting as necessary; then have the elephants return the peanuts to the bags before repeating the chant and having another elephant call out a number. After a few rounds, have the elephants and trainers switch places.

Elephant, Elephant raise your trunk high—
Way, way up to the sky.
How many peanuts for you today?
How many nuts can you stow away?

Jumbo Fun For Everyone

Give your little elephant trainers some estimating practice with this "pea-nutty" activity. Provide each youngster with an unshelled peanut. Invite each child to guess how many nuts are in his shell; then record his response. Invite all your little ones to open their peanuts, check their guesses, and then have a nutty time eating them! Challenge students further by providing two more peanuts for each child. Knowing how many peanuts were in one shell, can your little ones estimate how many peanuts will be in two shells?

Bring On The Clowns

Your youngsters are sure to fancy the funny faces in this visual-discrimination activity. To prepare, cut a clown's facial features and accessories (such as a bow tie or hat) from colorful felt. Cut enough features for two clown faces, making them different in shape and color. During circle time, use the felt cutouts to make a clown face on your flannelboard—excluding an eye, a nose, or another feature. Ask the children to determine what is missing from the clown. Continue by interchanging the felt pieces to make new faces. Or put features where they don't belong on the clown; then ask youngsters to identify what's wrong. Invite little ones to use the felt pieces to make their own crazy clown characters during free play.

Come Clown Around

Invite your youngsters to clown around with this pantomime performance. Teach youngsters the following song; then have them suggest things a clown might do in his circus act—such as make funny faces, ride a unicycle, or juggle balls. Encourage little ones to act out each suggested clown antic as they sing the song with you.

(sung to the tune of
"The Bear Went Over The Mountain")

Come clown around in the circus,
Come clown around in the circus,
Come clown around in the circus,
And entertain the crowd!

Circus Circle Of Fun!

Capture that big-top feeling during circle time by creating your very own three-ring circus! To prepare, place three plastic hoops or circles made from string on the floor. Invite three children to stand in the rings and perform a circus act, such as reciting the alphabet, counting to 20, or singing a special song. Have all three children perform the same act together. Introduce the performers as you announce the act with fanfare. You might say, "Ladies and gentlemen, let me present [Joey, Kaley, and Erin] singing 'The Clown Song.' " After the performance, encourage three more performers to get into the act!

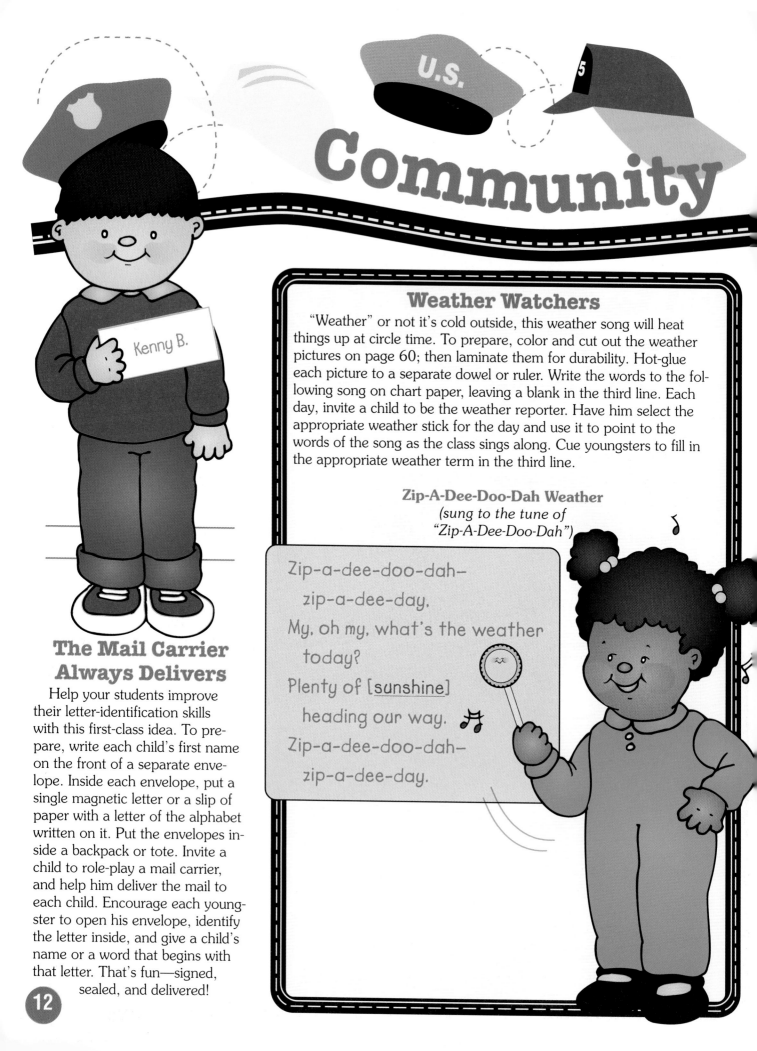

The Mail Carrier Always Delivers

Help your students improve their letter-identification skills with this first-class idea. To prepare, write each child's first name on the front of a separate envelope. Inside each envelope, put a single magnetic letter or a slip of paper with a letter of the alphabet written on it. Put the envelopes inside a backpack or tote. Invite a child to role-play a mail carrier, and help him deliver the mail to each child. Encourage each youngster to open his envelope, identify the letter inside, and give a child's name or a word that begins with that letter. That's fun—signed, sealed, and delivered!

Weather Watchers

"Weather" or not it's cold outside, this weather song will heat things up at circle time. To prepare, color and cut out the weather pictures on page 60; then laminate them for durability. Hot-glue each picture to a separate dowel or ruler. Write the words to the following song on chart paper, leaving a blank in the third line. Each day, invite a child to be the weather reporter. Have him select the appropriate weather stick for the day and use it to point to the words of the song as the class sings along. Cue youngsters to fill in the appropriate weather term in the third line.

Zip-A-Dee-Doo-Dah Weather
(sung to the tune of "Zip-A-Dee-Doo-Dah")

Zip-a-dee-doo-dah—
zip-a-dee-day,
My, oh my, what's the weather today?
Plenty of [sunshine] heading our way.
Zip-a-dee-doo-dah—
zip-a-dee-day.

Helpers

Dressed For Success

Dress up your show-and-tell time by inviting your youngsters to wear career-specific clothing. Encourage each child—on a specified day—to come to school dressed in the type of clothes that his mom, his dad, or a selected community helper wears to work. Ask parents to help their child find appropriate props and rehearse a description of the job for which he is dressed. Heigh-ho! Heigh-ho! It's off to work they go!

Undercover Careers

Uncover the careers of our community helpers with this mystery box. To prepare, collect items that indicate certain types of work, such as a firefighter's hat, a hammer, a stethoscope, or a whistle. Cover a box and its lid separately with Con-Tact® paper. Each day, secretly place one career item in the mystery box. Describe the item at circle time; then challenge the children to guess what it is and who uses it before revealing the undercover item.

Career Song

Help your youngsters describe some community helpers' jobs with this catchy career song.

Community Capers
(sung to the tune of "The Itsy-Bitsy Spider")

There are [firefighters] in our community.
They [put out fires] and they help you and me.

They're always there when there's a job to do.
So when you see a [firefighter], be sure to say, "Thank you!"

Repeat the song as many times as desired, substituting the careers and phrases below, or others your youngsters come up with.

police officers…direct the traffic
doctors…make us well
postal workers…deliver mail
farmers…grow our food

Dinosaurs

"Count-A-Saurus"

Teach the following dinosaur ditty to reinforce counting skills.

(sung to the tune of "Five Little Ducks")

One little dino went out to play,
Out in a muddy swamp one day.
He had such enormous fun.
He called for another dinosaur to come.

Two little dinos…
Three little dinos…
Four little dinos…

Five little dinos went out to play,
Out in a muddy swamp one day.
Then Mama called, "Come down the path!
It's time for you all to take a bubble bath!"

Directional Dinos

Direct your students to better math and language skills with this activity. Use the patterns on page 61 to cut a construction-paper dinosaur for each child. Distribute the dinosaurs; then verbally direct the children to place their dinosaurs under their chins, over their heads, behind their backs, etc. Be certain to emphasize each directional concept, such as *under* or *over*. Then have youngsters follow your lead as you silently position your dinosaur between your palms, on top of your knee, or beside your foot. Have students use directional words to describe where their dinosaurs are positioned. Before you know it, your students will have these language concepts *under* control!

A Daily Dose Of Dinosaur Math

You can count on dinosaurs to make daily math practice fun! Use the patterns on page 61 to cut several dinosaurs of each type from different colors of felt. During each day of your dinosaur unit, use the felt dinosaurs to reinforce a different math skill on your flannelboard. Have students count the dinosaurs as you place them on your flannelboard, then count backwards as you remove each dino. Encourage youngsters to sort the dinosaurs by color or type, then count the dinosaurs in each group. Reinforce ordinal numbers by displaying the dinosaurs in a line and asking the children to identify the dinosaur that is first, second, third, etc. Create a pattern featuring a sequence of colored dinosaurs or different types of dinosaurs; then have students extend the pattern. It's a prehistoric menagerie of math!

Calling All Dinosaurs

Greet each of your little dinos with this reptile roll call.

(sung to the tune of "Where Is Thumbkin?")

Teacher:	[Courtney]-a-saurus,
	[Courtney]-a-saurus…
Child:	Here I am. Here I am.
Teacher:	Hello, little dinosaur!
	Let me hear you stomp and roar!
	Come join in! Come join in!

grrrr

Red Dino, Red Dino, what do you see? I see an orange dino looking at me.

Dinosaur, Dinosaur

Teacher, Teacher, what do you see? You'll see youngsters working on color recognition when you use this variation on the text of Bill Martin, Jr.'s, *Brown Bear, Brown Bear, What Do You See?* (Henry Holt And Company, Inc.). To prepare, use the patterns on page 61 to cut dinosaurs from various colors of construction paper. (If desired, back each cutout with magnetic tape for display on a magnetic surface or with Velcro® for display on a flannelboard.) Then read the Bill Martin, Jr., story to your class. Once students are familiar with the repetitive text, use the dinosaur cutouts to create a "dino-mite" version of the story. Simply display one dinosaur cutout at a time, helping youngsters chime in with the rhyme.

To challenge more advanced students, substitute a set of white dinosaur cutouts labeled with color words.

Fairy Tales

"Sense-ible" Little Red Riding Hood

Use the story of "Little Red Riding Hood" to reinforce the five senses. Divide your class into two groups. Have one group recite Little Red Riding Hood's lines and the other group say the lines of the wolf disguised as Grandmother (see below). After the last line, have your little wolves jump up to surprise all your Little Red Riding Hoods!

Little Red Riding Hood:
"Grandmother, what big eyes you have!"
"Grandmother, what big ears you have!"
"Grandmother, what a big nose you have!"
"Grandmother, what big hands you have!"
"Grandmother, what big teeth you have!"

Wolf:
"The better to see you with, my dear!"
"The better to hear you with, my dear!"
"The better to smell you with, my dear!"
"The better to touch you with, my dear!"
"The better to eat you with!"

Fairy-Tale Association

Challenge your little ones to test their memories with this recall activity. In advance make a simple crown from construction paper. Seat the children in a circle; then name a fairy tale such as "Cinderella." Pass the crown to the child on your right. Have him put the crown on his head, name one character from "Cinderella," and then pass the crown to the next person. Continue until no other characters from that fairy tale can be named. Name another fairy tale and start again with the next child in the circle.

Prince Charming!

Name That Tale

When it's time to bring your fairy-tale unit to a close, "high-tale" it with the following verses. Challenge youngsters to identify the tales described in each verse. If desired, make up more verses for your other favorite fairy tales.

(sung to the tune of "Row, Row, Row Your Boat")

Once upon a time,
Two children in a wood
Came upon a candy house,
And, boy, did it look good!
(Hansel And Gretel)

Once upon a time,
A girl all dressed in red
Went to visit her granny,
But found a wolf instead.
(Little Red Riding Hood)

Once upon a time,
There lived a girl so fair.
She paid a visit to a home,
The home of the three bears.
(Goldilocks And The Three Bears)

Magic Counting Beans

Count on Jack's beans to show your students some magical math fun. In advance put ten dried beans, such as lima or kidney beans, into a paper cup for each child. Distribute the cups to the children. Secretly write down a numeral between 1 and 10 on a large piece of tagboard. Ask each child to guess the numeral he thinks is on the tagboard. Then have him count the same number of beans from his cup into the palm of his hand. Reveal the written numeral; then confirm whether any child guessed correctly. You can count on your youngsters wanting to do this again and again!

Snow White And Friends

Lead youngsters in this action poem as you role-play Snow White and her friends.

Bashful, Bashful, hide your face
Happy, Happy, dance in place.
Grumpy, Grumpy, make a frown.
Dopey, Dopey, turn around.
Sleepy, Sleepy, close your eyes.

Doc, Doc, you're so wise.
Sneezy, Sneezy, say, "Ah-choo!"
Snow White sure loves all of you!

Cover face with hands.
Dance.
Frown.
Twirl around.
Rest head on clasped hands and close eyes.
Tap temple and nod.
Pretend to sneeze.
Blow a kiss.

Fall Harvest

Pumpkin Patch

Invite your youngsters to join you in the pumpkin patch for this harvesttime fingerplay. Encourage your little ones to use their fingers to represent the five pumpkins, or use orange felt pumpkins on your flannelboard.

Five orange pumpkins growing on a vine,
"Thanks," said the farmer. "This one is fine."
Four orange pumpkins growing on the ground,
A coon ate one without a sound.
Three orange pumpkins under the sky,
"Yum," said the cook. "I'll make pumpkin pie."
Two orange pumpkins lying in the sun,
"Mine," said the baby, and then there was one.
One orange pumpkin left on the vine,
I'll take this one 'cause it's harvesttime!

Apple Of My Eye

Polish up critical-thinking skills with this apple game. Purchase a few apples of different colors, sizes, and varieties. Show the apples to the class and ask them to focus on the apples' colors, shapes, and sizes. Then discuss the similarities and differences among the apples. Next, introduce the game. Explain that you are thinking of one apple—the apple of your eye. Give clues to help youngsters determine which apple you've chosen. For example, say "My apple is not red." Guide a student volunteer to remove a red apple from the selection. Continue in this manner until only one apple remains. Then start the apple pickin' all over again!

Gourd Talk

Reap the benefits of this language activity as your youngsters go goo-goo over gourds! In advance collect gourds of interesting shapes and sizes in a basket. Have your students sit in a circle; then pass around one gourd at a time. Encourage the children to observe the gourds using their senses. Discuss the color, texture, and smell of each gourd. Ask your students to comment on each gourd's shape, size, and weight. As a further challenge, have youngsters determine the similarities and differences between the gourds. Then, during your next circle time, go on to "Groups Of Gourds" below.

Fall Picks

Here's a brainstorming activity that is worth pickin'! On chart paper draw a large apple. Invite students to brainstorm different food products that can be made with apples; then chart their responses inside the apple. When your apple list is complete, draw a large pumpkin on another piece of chart paper. Have the children list pumpkin foods and other purposes for pumpkins, such as making jack-o'-lanterns. Then ask each child to select a favorite item from each list. Put a tally mark next to each item each time it is selected. Total the tally marks to determine you class's favorite apple and pumpkin picks.

apple pie ||||| ||
apple juice |||||
apple butter ||||

Groups Of Gourds

Extend your exploration of gourds with this sorting game. Use yarn to make one large circle on the floor; then display a variety of gourds around the outside of the circle. Hold up a bumpy gourd and chant the rhyme below. Ask student volunteers to look for the bumpy gourds and place them inside the circle. Brainstorm together other ways to sort the gourds, such as by color, size, or shape. Once you have determined a new characteristic by which to sort, insert the characteristic into the rhyme. Continue grouping by other features in this gourd game of sorts.

Look! Look!
What do you see?
Find other gourds that are [bumpy] like me.

Family

We eat spaghetti at my house!

Mealtime Is Share Time

Gather together in a circle to share a tidbit or two about family mealtimes. Have your children pass a piece of play food around the circle as you recite the following poem. At the end of the verse, have the child holding the food item stand to share a story about a preferred family food, a mealtime custom, or a favorite mealtime story.

Oh, mealtime is sharing time;
We share food and stories and fun.
We talk and listen; eat and drink.
It's a great time for everyone!

You Can Always Count On Family

Count on family for fun! In advance cut a house shape from construction paper for each child—plus a few extras. Before circle time, ask each youngster to draw his family members "inside" a house. If a child splits his time between two residences, give him more than one house. Have him bring his drawing(s) to circle time to show and tell about his family. Then teach youngsters the following poem. Next begin counting and invite each youngster to stand when he hears the number that represents his family. Invite comparisons. Who has the smallest family? The largest?

How many people in your family?
How many special to you?
Stand when you hear the right number.
Don't forget to include YOU!

Go Camping

Go To The Park

Work Puzzles

Star Entertainment

Find out what families do for fun and frolic. To prepare, cut a small construction-paper star for each child. At circle time, discuss with your youngsters what they do with their families for fun; then list their responses on the chalkboard (leave plenty of room between responses). Give each child a star to tape next to the type of entertainment he most enjoys with his family. If desired, stretch this activity over the course of a few days. On separate days, have the students use the stars to show their favorite family activities that take place indoors, outdoors, and while on vacation. It's fun for the whole family!

The Chore Challenge

Doing chores is one way of helping each other in a family. Help youngsters make a list of typical chores they do at home. From the list, vote on one chore that all the children could do to help their families. Decide on the number of days the chore is to be done. Then write a short parent note that states the designated chore and the number of days the children have agreed to do it. Include a line for parents to sign when the chore is completed. Ask students to return the signed notes to school at the end of the designated period. Then watch your youngsters "chore-tle" with delight as you award them with ribbons for a task well done!

Family Love Song

Sing this loving song with your children to underscore the key element of families—love. Once youngsters have learned the words to the song, have them sing it for their families at home.

You Are My Family
(sung to the tune of "You Are My Sunshine")

You are my family, my loving family.
I feel so happy living with you.
You are so special, so very special!
Thanks for loving me the way you do.

Teach this second verse to show your little ones that your class is a special family, too.

You are my family, my preschool family,
I feel so happy right here with you.
With you I play, sing, and learn so many things.
Thanks for loving me the way you do.

The Farm

Chores Round The Farm

Plant the seeds for better listening skills with this barnyard version of Telephone. First discuss the many types of chores a farmer does, such as milking the cow, driving the tractor, and seeding the fields. With your students sitting in a circle, whisper a chore in one child's ear. Then ask him to speak clearly as he whispers that same chore into the ear of the person to his right. Can the chore get passed around the circle successfully? Whether it does or not, invite everyone to act out the chore you named. Then continue to pass different chores until all the work gets done round the farm!

A Farmer's Life For Me

Get your students thinking about the life of a farmer with this ABC poem. As you recite the following poem, pass around a farm-related item, such as a packet of seeds, a plastic farm animal, or a toy tractor. At the end of the poem, have the child holding the farm item tell what he would like the most about living on a farm and what he would like the least. Recite the poem as many times as desired. Perhaps each of your youngsters will agree—"Farm living is the life for me!"

A-b-c-d-e-f-g,
A farmer's life is so busy.
H-i-j-k-l-and-m,
He goes from daybreak 'til day's end.
N-o-p-q-r-s-t,
Think how busy your life would be,
U-v-w-x-y-z,
If you lived on a farm with your family!

Designer Coats

Invite your little ones to design new coats for some favorite farm animals. Cut a large sheep, turkey, and cow from poster board. Display the cutouts on a wall or bulletin board within children's reach. Put a container of cotton balls under the sheep, a container of feathers under the turkey, and a container of quarter-sized paper circles under the cow. Select a student volunteer to stand in front of each animal. Give each volunteer a card with a numeral from 1 to 5 written on it; then have him count out the corresponding number of items from the container below his animal. Check each child for accuracy. Then brush glue onto a portion of each animal and have each child adhere his counted items. Repeat the activity until all your little designers have added to these new designer coats.

Countdown At The Henhouse

This countdown rhyme is "eggs-actly" what the teacher ordered!

[Five] little eggs all snug in a nest.
[Five] chicks inside are all at rest.

Peck, peck, peck—what's that I hear?
One little chick will soon appear!

Four little eggs…
Three little eggs…
Two little eggs…
One little egg…

Hold up [five] fingers.
Close hand and cover
*   with other fist.*

Pop one finger out of fist.

Funny Farm Sounds

You'll hear a "moo-moo" here and an "oink-oink" there with this animal-sounds game. In advance gather a picture of a farm animal for each child, and place each picture in an individual envelope. Distribute the envelopes, encouraging each child to keep his envelope's contents a secret. Next give each child a turn to make the sound of his farm animal; then challenge classmates to identify the animal. Once everyone has had a turn, make a chorus of farm-animal sounds together.

The Five Senses

Sailing The Deep "See"

Make youngsters aware of their amazing sense of sight with this "deep-see" activity. In advance prepare a large batch of blue gelatin in a clear glass or plastic bowl. Cut a variety of alphabet letters (ones your students can identify) from blue construction paper. Place the letters in an envelope; then set the bowl of set gelatin and the envelope on the floor in your circle area. Explain that each child will have a turn to look into the deep blue sea (the gelatin) to see if she can see anything at the bottom.

Slip a letter beneath the bowl. Then teach youngsters this song:

Some Children Went To Sea
(sung to the tune of "A Sailor Went To Sea")

Some children went to sea-sea-sea
To see what they could see-see-see.
They saw the letter [R - R - R]
At the bottom of the deep sea-sea-sea!

Invite a few children to gather around the bowl and see what they can see at the bottom of the sea. Once they have correctly identified the letter, sing the song, inserting the name of the letter into the third line. Repeat the activity until every child has had a turn to "see-see-see" a letter.

Touch And Go

Don't pass up this activity that explores the sense of touch. To prepare, gather several items with interesting textures, such as a tennis ball, a small stuffed animal, or a shell. Put one item in a large grocery bag and fold the top over. At circle time, have youngsters pass the bag as you sing the following song:

Pass, Pass, Pass The Bag
(sung to the tune of "Row, Row, Row Your Boat")

Pass, pass, pass the bag,
Round and round it goes.
What could be inside it now?
What do you suppose?

When you stop singing, have the child holding the bag reach inside to feel and guess its contents. Remind the child not to peek! After he announces his guess, have the next child in the circle display the item for all to see. Repeat this touch-and-go game with additional items.

Now Hear This!

Your students are bound to shout, "Hear! Hear!" to this listening activity! In advance tape-record each child speaking. Ask each youngster to repeat a specified sentence, or record the children's candid conversations throughout the course of a day. In the days that follow, play the tape to see if the children can identify their own voices and those of their classmates. What an earful of fun!

Colorful Cuisine

Add a little color to your study of the five senses with this taste test. In advance add enough red food coloring to a half-gallon of milk to tint it pink; then pour a small cup of pink milk for each child. Next mix cream cheese with blue food coloring and spread it on a minibagel for each child. Display the bagels and milk during circle time, and tell your youngsters they will be invited to try these treats during snacktime. Ask them if they think they will like the taste of the pink milk and blue cream cheese; then chart their responses. After snack, record their responses to these colorful culinary treats. Did their reactions match their predictions?

A "Scent-sible" Match

"Odor" up some fun with this matching game. To prepare, program a card for each child with a smiley face on one side and a frowning face on the other. Next cut three bottle shapes from construction paper. Gather three fragrant items, such as cinnamon, orange extract, and cocoa powder. Rub a different fragrance onto each paper bottle to transfer the scent. Then put some cinnamon, a few orange wedges, and a chocolate candy bar in separate lunch bags. During circle time, distribute the programmed cards. Pass one paper bottle for all students to smell. Then pass one lunch bag. Ask your youngsters to determine whether or not the scent in the bag matches the scent on the bottle. If they decide the scents match, have them hold their cards with the smiley faces toward you. If they decide the scents are different, have them display the frowning sides of their cards. Continue the game until each scent has met its match. Then reveal each bag's contents.

Friends

Friendship Bears

This flannelboard activity "bears" repeating! In advance, cut five simple bear shapes from each of two different colors of felt. During circle time, tell a friendship story that emphasizes the concept of patterning. For example, "A group of bear friends went hiking. A red bear led the group. A blue bear was second. A red bear was third, and a blue bear was fourth." As you tell the story, have student volunteers put the felt bears on a flannelboard in the order described. Ask youngsters to review the pattern; then have more children continue the pattern using all the bears. Continue by describing other friendly outings, such as the bear friends lining up for a movie or ice cream.

Circle Of Friends

Invite your youngsters to create a circle of friends. To prepare, gather a number of different wallpaper samples equal to half the children in your class. Make a tagboard pattern of a person; then use it to trace and cut two people from each wallpaper sample. Before circle time, distribute the wallpaper cutouts. Instruct each child to find the classmate who has the matching cutout and sit next to him in the circle. Once the pairs are seated, demonstrate how to interview a partner by asking a designated question such as, "What is your favorite color?" Then have each friendly pair introduce each other and share the results of the interview.

Each day during your friendship unit, repeat this activity with new pairs and different interview questions.

Paper Pals

Keep eyes and ears on you as you snip your way through this story with a surprise ending. In advance fold a 6" x 18" piece of construction paper in half twice so that it measures 4 1/2" x 6". Draw a simple paper-doll figure on the folded paper as shown, making sure the arms go off the edges of the paper. As you begin, keep the drawing facing you and the blank side facing the children. Starting at one leg, begin to slowly cut along the lines of the doll as you make up a story about an imaginary child on her first day of school. Tell about the child meeting classmates on the school playground and at centers. Be certain not to cut apart the folds. As you complete cutting the doll from paper, wrap up the story by telling how the child had made many new friends by the end of the day. Then unfold the paper to display a row of paper pals!

The Teacher's Friend

Invite an adult friend of yours to come to your classroom and sing the praises of friendship. Have your youngsters sit in a semicircle; then sit beside your friend in the front. Talk about how you met. Tell a favorite story about your friendship. If possible, show photographs of special moments you've shared together. Discuss the importance of listening, laughing, and forgiving in a friendship. Lessons about friendship will come naturally, and children will be delighted to discover that teachers can be good friends, too.

Where's Rodney?

Friendly Faces

Help little ones get to know names and faces with this memory game. Seat all the children in a circle; then have an adult helper escort one child out of sight and out of earshot from the rest of the class. Quietly direct another child in the circle to hide himself in a designated spot. Invite the first child back into the circle; then chant the following:

Friends, friends, one, two, three.
Someone is hiding—
Who can it be?

Give the child a moment to scan her classmates and decide who is hiding. If she is uncertain, give clues until she is successful. After the hidden child reveals himself, begin the game again with two new players.

Garden

Farmer In The Garden

Harvest language skills as you play this veggie version of The Farmer In The Dell. In advance make a vegetable necklace for each child. Duplicate a class supply of the vegetable patterns on page 62 onto colored construction paper; then cut them out. To make a necklace, punch a hole in the top of one vegetable cutout, thread a length of yarn through the hole, and knot the ends together. Distribute a necklace to each child and have him identify the vegetable on his necklace.

Have the students stand in a circle. Call one child to the center. Designate him as the farmer and give him a straw hat to wear. As you sing the following song, encourage the farmer to pick a child to join him in the circle and then insert the name of the vegetable that child is wearing into the song. Have all the children wearing that vegetable come to the center. Continue until all the vegetables have been picked. After singing the final verse, have students swap necklaces and send a new farmer veggie pickin'.

The farmer in the garden,
The farmer in the garden,
Heigh-ho, the veggie-o,
The farmer in the garden.

The farmer picks [potatoes].
The farmer picks [potatoes].
Heigh-ho, the veggie-o,
The farmer picks [potatoes].

Final verse
The farmer in the garden,
The farmer in the garden,
Heigh-ho, the veggie-o,
Harvesttime is here!

Mystery Veggie

It's no mystery—this activity will strengthen youngsters' critical-thinking skills! To prepare, duplicate and cut out the vegetable patterns on page 62. Each day during your garden unit, seal one fresh vegetable (one that is represented in the vegetable pictures) inside a shoebox. Display three of the vegetable pictures, including the one that represents the vegetable in the box. Pass the box around the circle. As you chant the following rhyme, have each child shake the box to get a sense of the vegetable's size, weight, and shape. Encourage students to comment about these characteristics. Once all the children have held the box, invite youngsters to guess which of the three vegetables is inside the box. Then reveal the mystery vegetable.

Something from the garden,
Which veggie can it be?
Listen to the sound it makes,
Before we look to see.

Today is [Tuesday]

What is growing in my garden today?

In my garden, I have

Read All About It!

Grow a crop of readers with this daily prereading activity. To prepare, cut pictures of several different (familiar) vegetables and flowers from seed catalogs. (Or you might substitute copies of the vegetable patterns on page 62 for the pictures of vegetables.) Write the sentences below on a sheet of chart paper. Decorate the edges of the paper with drawings of flowers and vegetables if desired. Laminate the chart paper for repeated use. Next, write each day of the week on a separate tagboard strip, sized to fit on the first blank on your chart.

Each day during circle time, ask a student volunteer to tape the appropriate day-of-the-week strip to the chart. Then have her select a cutout and tape it to the chart as well. Encourage youngsters to identify the flower or vegetable selected. Then read the chart together, pointing to the words as you read.

Today is _____.
What is growing in my garden today?
In my garden, I have _____.

Something Big From Something Small

Any way you slice it, this activity provides a fruitful science experience. Present a melon and a peach to your class. Discuss the size of each fruit. Ask youngsters to make some predictions about the seeds inside each fruit. Which fruit will have the larger seeds? Which will have smaller seeds? Then cut open the melon and scoop a spoonful of seeds onto a paper towel. Cut open the peach, remove the pit, and lay the pit next to the melon seeds. Talk about your students' predictions. Then brainstorm other examples of small fruits with large seeds, such as cherries, or large fruits with small seeds, such as grapefruit. Help students conclude that the size of the seed is not determined by the size of the fruit.

Bloomin' Bulb

Measurement skills will bloom as your little ones observe the growth of a bulb. Purchase a sprouted bulb from your local garden center. Gather a container of linking cubes and program a sheet of chart paper with the title "How Big Is Our Bulb?" At circle time, present the bulb to your class and explain that the children are going to measure the plant. Ask a student volunteer to connect enough linking cubes to equal the height of the plant; then count aloud the number of cubes used. Divide the class into pairs and have each pair connect the same number of cubes. Have each pair look for classroom items that equal the length of the cubes. Invite the children to bring the items to the circle. Attach those items that are lightweight to the chart paper. If children find items that are too heavy or immovable, write the names of those items on the chart. Repeat this activity periodically as your bulb continues to grow. Later, transplant the bulb outdoors to beautify your school or center grounds.

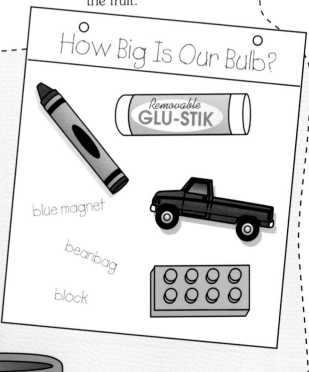

How Big Is Our Bulb?

Removable GLU-STIK

blue magnet

beanbag

block

Health & Safety

Sneaky Snack

Give your students practice selecting foods that promote good dental health. Show the children a variety of fruits and vegetables that are good for teeth—such as a carrot, an apple, or a celery stick. Then display samples of foods that are not so good for teeth—such as a candy bar, jelly beans, or a cookie. Collect all of the food items in a basket. Tell your students you need their help in identifying the sugary snacks that are sneaking their way into your collection of healthful snacks. Display three snacks at a time: two that represent good dental-health choices and one that represents a poor choice. Ask the children to identify the sneaky, sugary snack. Continue until you've eliminated all the sweets from your treats.

Counting With The Tooth Fairy

Practice counting and listening skills with the help of some tooth-fairy magic. Put aside a small bell. Place one plastic cup and five Styrofoam® peanuts—to represent teeth—in front of each child. Invite the children to pretend they are tooth fairies. Explain that the tooth fairies are going on a tooth-collecting trip. Have the children count the number of times they hear you ring the bell and place the corresponding number of teeth in their cups. Check for accuracy by asking each child to count the number of teeth he has in his cup. With each house the tooth fairies visit, have them empty their cups and listen for a different number of teeth to collect.

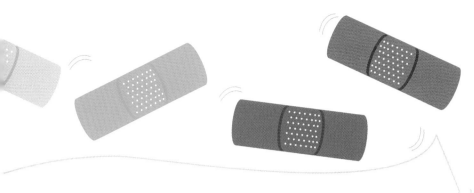

Get Up & Go

Wake your kids up to some fire-safety rules. Purchase an inexpensive battery-operated smoke alarm. (Or make a paper model from a white paper plate with a red construction-paper button.) With a puppet on one hand, ask the students to observe the puppet to see if it knows what to do in a fire. Push the test button to sound the alarm; then make the puppet hide beneath your arm. Encourage the children to convince the puppet that hiding is the wrong thing to do. Stress this rule: in case of a fire, get out and stay out! To reinforce this lesson, teach the children the following song. Then have them pretend to be sleeping while you sound the alarm again. Line up to practice leaving the building.

Fire-Safety Song
(sung to the tune of "Are You Sleeping?")

While you're sleeping,
While you're sleeping,
Beep! Beep! Beep!
Beep! Beep! Beep!
The smoke alarm is ringing.
The smoke alarm is ringing.
Out of bed!
Move your feet!

Brush Your Teeth

Teach your youngsters to take the time that is necessary to have a fresh, bright smile. Set a small sand timer or kitchen timer before the children. Explain that to do a complete job of brushing, it is best to brush for three minutes. Then use a pretzel stick as a toothbrush to demonstrate how to brush your teeth properly. Give each child his own pretzel stick, set the timer, and lead the children in a three-minute brushing session. Then invite your little dental students to eat their makeshift toothbrushes!

Hello, 911?

Practice dialing 911 in this role-playing activity that's a lifesaver. Write "911" in large numerals on your chalkboard. Bring two toy telephones to circle time: one for yourself and one for a child. Discuss the importance of calling 911 in an emergency. Create an emergency scenario and explain it to the class. Select one child to dial "911" and report the emergency to you—the dispatcher—as you listen on the other phone. Encourage the child to speak clearly and to give her full name and address. Then give her a certificate that says "I'm number one at calling 911." Provide other youngsters with the opportunity to practice emergency calls during fire-safety week.

Leaves

Leaves In Action

"Leaf" it to this action rhyme to help little ones learn about opposites. To prepare, use the leaf patterns on page 60 to cut a class supply of construction-paper leaves. Glue each leaf to a craft stick. Give each child a leaf puppet; then lead the class in motions to accompany this rhyme:

The leaves are high.
The leaves are low.
The leaves are blowing soft and slow.

The leaves are up.
The leaves are down.
The leaves are blowing all around.

The leaves are here.
The leaves are there.
The leaves are blowing everywhere.

Would You Eat A Leaf?

yes	no
Maria	J. T.
am	Cherlanda
	Emma

Incredible Edible Leaves

Your youngsters will have a hard time "be-leaf-ing" that some leaves are edible. In advance make a chart titled "Would You Eat A Leaf?" Under the title, make a "Yes" column and a "No" column. Ask each child to respond to the question on the chart by placing a sticky note labeled with his name in the corresponding column. Next show children a head of iceberg lettuce, and ask them if they have eaten lettuce in a salad or on a hamburger. As you peel the lettuce off the head, explain that each layer is actually a leaf. Invite children to change their responses on the chart now that they understand that insects aren't the only ones that lunch on leaves.

Problems With Leaves

Even your littlest learners can add and subtract when they use some leafy manipulatives! To prepare, use the leaf patterns on page 60 to cut a supply of construction-paper leaves. Sketch a bare tree on brown craft paper for a storyboard. Then read aloud the rhyming word problems below, inserting numbers appropriate for your little ones' abilities. Invite youngsters to use the paper leaves and the tree to solve the problems.

Addition Rhyme:
One little leaf is on the tree.
___ leaves are on the ground.
Put them all together now.
How many have you found?

Subtraction Rhyme:
___ autumn leaves were on the
    tree.
The wind blew ___ away.
Look at the tree and tell me,
    please,
How many leaves did stay?

Summer Leaves, Autumn Leaves

Rake in a science lesson by asking youngsters to sort summer and autumn leaves. If you are able, collect enough green leaves and colorful fall leaves to give each child one leaf. (Or cut green, orange, and red leaves from construction paper.) Divide a sheet of chart paper in half; then label one column "Summer" and the other column "Autumn."

Distribute the leaves. Explain that leaves contain *chlorophyll*—a special chemical that helps the leaf turn sunlight, water, and air into food for the tree. It also makes leaves look green. In summer, the leaves make a lot of food for the tree. But in autumn (when there is less sunlight, drier weather, and cooler air), the chlorophyll goes away and the tree gets ready to rest for the winter. When the chlorophyll goes away, the leaf isn't green anymore. It shows its true colors, such as red and orange. After your explanation, ask each child to look at her leaf and decide if it is a summer leaf or an autumn leaf. Help her attach her leaf to the chart in the appropriate column.

"That's My Leaf!"

Watch observation skills branch out as your little ones take a close look at leaves. Encourage each child to bring an autumn leaf from home; have a few extras on hand for children who need them. Invite each child to show his leaf to the class. Next call out a descriptive word such as *red,* and then ask all the children with red leaves to hold their leaves high and announce, "That's my leaf!" Continue to call out other adjectives, such as *speckled, pointed,* or *smooth.*

New Year

There's A New Year In The Air!

Give your students the "write" stuff for the new year. In advance make a New Year's banner that says "WELCOME [1999]!" Display the banner, and have youngsters identify the letters and numerals on it. Model how to read the name of the new year. Demonstrate how to use an index finger to write in the air. Then encourage the children to follow your lead in writing each letter and numeral from the banner in the air. For added fun, air-write other numerals, letters, or names of classmates.

Countdown To A New Year

Set the stage for a simulation of the Times Square countdown. To prepare, tape colorful crepe-paper streamers to a beach ball. Add numeral cutouts to form the new year's number. During circle time, pretend the countdown to midnight is only moments away. Have youngsters use their fingers to practice counting down from ten. After the children have practiced several times, have them stand to get ready for the drop of the New Year ball. Hold the beach ball up in the air. As you begin to count backward, slowly lower the ball. Encourage youngsters to gradually lower their bodies to the floor in unison with the ball. When you have reached the number one and the ball has touched the floor, have the children leap into the air and yell, "Happy New Year!"

A Noisy New Year

Make these nifty noisemakers to accompany the New Year songs on this page. In advance gather a class supply of film canisters from a local film processor. Cut three 18-inch lengths of ribbon or crepe paper for each child. Purchase a bag of dried black-eyed peas; then put the peas at a table with the film canisters and ribbon. Invite one small group of children at a time to make their noisemakers. Have each child count ten peas into a film canister. Instruct her to drape the ribbons over the opening of the canister, then snap the cap on with the ribbons caught beneath it. Ready? Set? Shake!

Singin' A New Year's Tune

Invite youngsters to use their noisemakers (see "A Noisy New Year") and their voices to welcome the new year with a tune or two.

Happy New Year To You!
(sung to the tune of "Happy Birthday To You")

Happy birthday, New Year.
Happy birthday, New Year.
Happy birthday, [1999].
Happy birthday, New Year.
HAPPY NEW YEAR!
(Shout the last line.)

A Brand New Year Is Here!
(sung to the tune of "Go Tell It On The Mountain")

Go tell it on the mountain,
Over the hill and everywhere.
Go tell it on the mountain,
A brand new year is here!
[1999!]
(Cup hands around mouth and shout year.)

Celebration Station

What's missing from your New Year's celebration? Find out with this visual-discrimination activity. Collect several varied New Year's party supplies—such as a party hat, a noisemaker, a bag of confetti, a roll of party streamers, and a horn. Display the party items in front of the children. Have the children identify each item and its purpose. Then put the featured items in a large box. Take all but one of the items back out and display them again. Can your youngsters determine which object is missing?

Exciting Reciting

Spruce up Mother Goose with some varied voices! Recite rhymes using special voices, such as Old King Cole's majestic voice, Little Boy Blue's sleepy voice, and Mother Goose's elderly voice. Can the children think of other voices to use? Memorizing nursery rhymes has never been so much fun!

Rhyme Time

Help little ones identify rhyming words with this cloze activity. After youngsters have become familiar with a nursery rhyme, such as "Little Miss Muffet," stop before a selected rhyming word while reciting it. Then wait for the children to provide the missing word. For instance, you might say, "Little Miss Muffet sat on a…" Then stop to allow the class to say, "tuffet." Once the children have memorized the rhyme, say one line; then signal the class to supply the following line. Continue until the entire rhyme has been recited.

Rhyme Review

A-tisket, a-tasket, a rhyme review in a basket! In a basket, collect items to represent the nursery rhymes you have studied, such as a plastic sheep for "Little Bo-Peep," a plastic egg for "Humpty Dumpty," and a candle for "Jack Be Nimble." Tell your little ones that Mother Goose left a basket to help them remember her rhymes. Then have one child at a time select an item from Mother Goose's basket. Help the child to identify the nursery rhyme that the item represents. Then have the child lead the class in reciting that rhyme.

"Jack be nimble..."

Name That Tune!

Try this nursery-rhyme version of Name That Tune. Many nursery rhymes such as "Mary Had a Little Lamb," "Baa, Baa, Black Sheep," and "Hickory, Dickory, Dock" have been set to music. Hum the tunes from these rhymes and others like them; then challenge your youngsters to identify the rhymes. After you've experimented with humming, lead little ones in clapping, snapping, or even tongue-clicking the rhythms of familiar rhymes. It's a rhythm-and-rhyme good time!

Reading Rhymes

Use nursery-rhyme collections to give your little ones some experience with context clues. Gather a few books that feature a collection of Mother Goose rhymes. As you slowly preview each book together, ask youngsters to carefully observe the illustrations. Challenge the class to identify each rhyme from the picture clues. Discuss the items that they recognize. If they have difficulty naming a rhyme, provide clues to assist them.
Lead the class in reciting each rhyme as it is identified.

"Look! The cat and the fiddle!"

Nutrition

Tune In To Food

Tune your little ones in to the six food groups with this song. Duplicate and cut apart the food cards on page 63. Make one card for each child. (You may want to color the food pictures.) Review the six food groups and help each child identify the group to which his food belongs. Then invite the children to sing the first verse of the following song with you. As you sing the remaining verses to the children, have them listen carefully and raise their food cards to correspond with the verses.

If You're Hungry
(sung to the tune of "If You're Happy And You Know It")

If you're hungry and you know it, clap your hands. *(Clap twice.)*
If you're hungry and you know it, clap your hands. *(Clap twice.)*
If you're hungry and you know it,
Then your tummy's sure to show it.

(Pause to make a growling sound.)

If you're hungry and you know it, clap your hands. *(Clap twice.)*

If you have a grain food, show us now.
If you have a grain food, show us now.
Look at your card, please do.
Is it something good for you?
If you have a grain food, show us now.

Continue with verses about dairy, protein, fruit, veggie, and fatty foods.

Food Clues

Serve up a healthy review of colors and shapes with this riddle game. Duplicate and cut apart the food cards on page 63. Color at least one card for each child. Share the following riddle with the class: "I am red. I am round. I am a fruit. What am I?" Challenge the children to solve the riddle. Next distribute the food cards. Create another riddle with clues that describe a food card held by one of the children. Describe the mystery food's color, shape, and food group. Instruct the child who is holding the solution to the riddle to stand and show her card for all to see. Continue the guessing game until each child has solved a riddle.

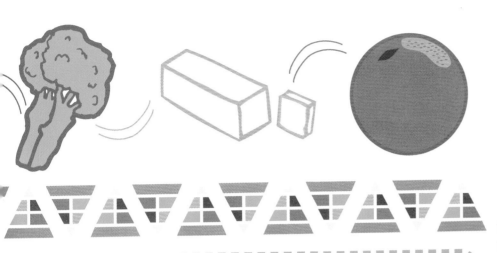

Balanced Sandwiches

Challenge your little nutritionists to design a well-balanced sandwich. With a picture of the Food Guide Pyramid in full view, discuss the types of foods that belong to each food group. Ask youngsters to decide which of these foods might go into a healthful sandwich. Encourage them to work together to create a sandwich with items from each of the food groups. Draw a large picture of the sandwich as it develops. Does everyone agree that the sandwich is well balanced? Does everyone agree that it would be tasty? If desired, share *your* idea of a balanced sandwich by making an actual sub with the class. Have the ingredients ready and invite student volunteers to add layers to the sandwich. Then cut the sub into enough small squares for each child to have a "snackwich."

Pyramid Match

Work on classification skills with this food-matching activity. In advance design a large model of the Food Guide Pyramid using the following colors of construction paper: brown for grains, green for vegetables, yellow for fruits, white for dairy, red for proteins, and blue for fats. Duplicate and cut apart the food cards on page 63. If desired, program the back of each card with a construction-paper circle to correspond to the color of its food group on the pyramid. Have the class sit in a circle; then place the Food Guide Pyramid in the center. Give each child a food card. Invite each child to name the food on her card and place it on the corresponding section of the pyramid. If needed, invite younger children to use the colored circles on the backs of their cards to help them make their matches.

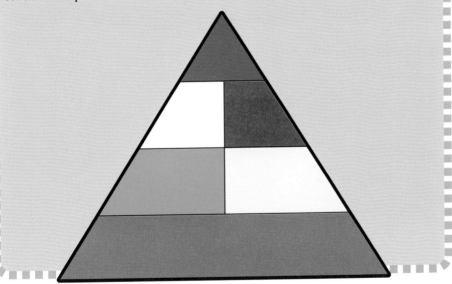

Labeled Nutrition

Your students will label this activity "lots of fun" as they categorize their favorite foods into the six food groups. Ask parents to send to school a package label from one of their child's favorite foods. Have your youngsters bring their labels to circle time. Divide a length of bulletin-board paper into six sections; then write across the top "Our Favorite Foods From The Food Groups." Ask each youngster to identify the food group to which his label belongs. Then have him tape his label to the appropriate section of the chart. In which food group do most of your students have a favorite food? If desired, have students draw pictures of their favorite foods from the food groups that are least represented; then label them and add them to the chart.

Ocean

Is it a shovel?

Something's Fishy!

Fishing for a new way to build vocabulary? Then dive right into this descriptive activity. In advance collect several beach items, such as a pair of sunglasses, a bottle of sunblock, or a sand pail and shovel. Put one of these items in a beach bag. During circle time, describe the item that is inside the bag and ask youngsters to guess what object you are describing. Continue to play this guessing game by changing the item inside the bag. In the days that follow, invite each child to bring to school a beach item of his choice to place in the mystery bag. Then help him provide clues to help the class name the mystery object.

Songs By The Seashore

Use this seaworthy song to strengthen prereading skills. To prepare, copy the words of the song below on chart paper. Then gather pictures of ocean-related items, such as a shell, a dolphin, or a starfish. Invite a youngster to select a picture; then hold the picture over the blanks on the chart to complete each line of the song. To shovel up some added fun, use a sand shovel to point to the words as you sing along.

Bring It Back!
(sung to the tune of
"My Bonnie Lies Over The Ocean")

My ____ lies under the ocean.
My ____ lies under the sea.
My ____ lies under the ocean.
Oh! Bring back my ____ to me.

(Optional)
Bring back! Bring back!
Oh! Bring back my ____ to me, to me.
Bring back! Bring back!
Oh! Bring back my ____ to me.

Famished Fish

Create commotion by the ocean as you take a bite out of subtraction with this countdown rhyme. As you recite the rhyme, have little ones use their fingers to symbolize each number of fish.

Out in the middle of the ocean so
  deep,
[Five] little fish swim and leap.
Along comes a shark…
GULP!

(Continue to repeat the first verse using four little fish, three little fish, and two little fish. Then end the rhyme with the verse that follows.)

Out in the middle of the ocean so
  deep,
One little fish started to weep.
Along came a shark
And said, "I'm full!"

Follow up the fingerplay with this variation. Give each child five Goldfish® crackers to use as manipulatives. As you recite the rhyme again, have each little shark feed on a fish each time he says, "GULP!"

Hmm, I think it's a shark!

Sock It To 'Em!

Put your little beachcombers' senses to the test with this activity. In advance collect pairs of shells similar in shape and size or pairs of rubber sea creatures, such as fish, crabs, or sharks. Have your youngsters sit in a circle; then place one item from each pair of objects in the center. Pass the remaining items for the children to see and touch; then collect them. Without the children seeing, place one of these items inside a sock. Tie a loose knot in the end of the sock, and then pass it around the circle. Ask each child to describe how the hidden object feels. Next challenge youngsters to point to the object in the center of the circle that matches the item in the sock.

"Sea-sational" Graphing

The loose ends of your ocean unit will be "tide" together with this graphing activity. Draw a simple bar graph on poster board. If desired, scallop the top of the poster board to resemble waves. Ask each child to name her favorite sea creature. At the bottom of the graph, make a simple drawing of each type of ocean animal named. Provide small photographs of each child or small sticky notes labeled with each child's name to use as graph markers. Have each child place her photo or sticky note above her favorite sea animal. Now your youngsters' ocean favorites will not be forgotten!

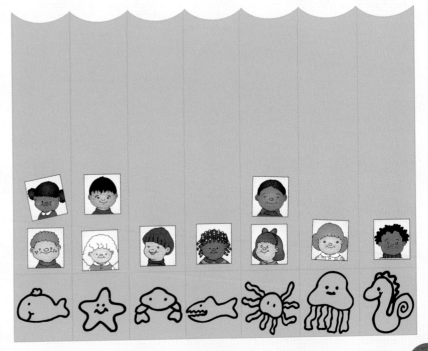

Rain

Rain—Friend Or Foe?

Chase away the rainy-day blues with this language activity that will have everyone thinking happy thoughts about rain. Inflate a large blue balloon; then introduce it to the class as a raindrop. Have your youngsters sit in a circle, then pass the raindrop as you repeatedly sing the traditional song "Rain, Rain, Go Away." Insert each child's name in the song as he holds the balloon.

Next ask youngsters if they enjoy the rain or wish it would go away. Discuss the activities they enjoy doing inside and outside on a rainy day. Then ask students to think about the good things rain provides for people and the earth. Pass the balloon raindrop around again. As each child holds the balloon, encourage him to share one good thing about the rain.

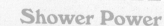

Note: Balloons can be a choking hazard for small children. Provide close supervision.

Shower Power

Use seedlings to demonstrate the importance of rain. Purchase two small seedlings from a nursery. Tape a blue paper raindrop to one seedling's pot. Explain to your youngsters that this plant will be given water from a watering can, to simulate rain. Tape a blue raindrop with a black slash mark through it on the second seedling's pot. Explain that this plant will not be given water, to simulate dry weather. Provide a watering can for a volunteer to water the first plant, and then set both seedlings on a windowsill. Ask your youngsters to predict what will happen after a few days. Each day for several days, observe the plants and the changes that are taking place. Water the first plant daily. After several days it will be obvious that rain showers make happy flowers! Extend the lesson by giving a dose of water to the second plant and observing its improvement.

The Colors Of The Rainbow

Find a lesson on colors when you look over this rainbow! In advance cut three-foot streamers from red, orange, yellow, green, blue, and purple crepe paper. Write the corresponding color words on large index cards. Give each child one streamer and have him identify the color. Once everyone has a streamer, display one index card and announce the color word. Have all the children with streamers of that color gather together in a designated spot. Repeat this process with the other colors until all youngsters have been grouped. Then put on some instrumental music, and invite all the colors of the rainbow to move freely around your classroom.

Rainmaker

Make it rain in the classroom with this easy science demonstration. Seat children in a semicircle, so they can watch the rainstorm from a safe distance. Fill a Crock-Pot® with water; then set it on a small table in front of your group. Plug in the Crock-Pot® and boil the water. Fill an aluminum pie plate with ice cubes and hold it over the steaming water. Observe together as the steam touches the cold pie plate, condenses into water drops, and then falls down like rain. It's a drip-drop drama!

Weather Watch

The forecast for this weather activity is developing skills with observation, recording data, and comparing data! Create a monthly weather graph by dividing a sheet of chart paper into three columns labeled "Sunny," "Rainy," and "Cloudy." Draw a corresponding symbol next to each label. Select one child each day to be the weather watcher; then sing the following weather song. Have the weather watcher look out the window, give a weather report, and then draw an "x" in the column that best represents the weather for the day. At the end of the month, count and compare the number of sunny, cloudy, and rainy days.

(sung to the tune of "Where Is Thumbkin?")
Weather watcher,
Weather watcher,
Look outside,
Look outside,
Tell us what the weather's like,
Tell us what the weather's like,
Sun, rain, clouds?
Sun, rain, clouds?

43

Self-Awareness

Kool Kids

Celebrate individual choices with this graphing activity. Purchase a large box of Popsicles® with three flavors. Label a sheet of chart paper "Our Favorite Popsicles®;" then divide the paper into three rows. Draw a colored Popsicle® representing one flavor in each row. Present the different Popsicle® flavors to your class; then have each child come forward and select the flavor of his choice. Invite the children to eat their cool treats as you call their attention to the different choices they made. Distribute wet wipes for cleaning hands and Popsicle® sticks. Then invite one child at a time to tape his stick to the row on the graph that represents the flavor he selected. Tally the results; then remind youngsters that it's cool to make their own choices!

Our Favorite Popsicles

orange	‖
cherry	‖‖‖‖‖
grape	‖‖‖‖

Warm Fuzzy

Make your youngsters feel warm and fuzzy all over! In advance make a fuzzy critter for each of your students. To make one, cut a two-inch square of Con-Tact® paper into a heart shape to serve as feet. Glue tiny wiggle eyes to a large cotton ball; then glue the cotton ball to the nonstick side of the Con-Tact®-paper feet. During circle time, select a child to come forward. Peel the backing from the Con-Tact® paper, and stick the fuzzy critter on the child's shoulder as you give him a hug. Say, "Here's a warm fuzzy from me to you!" Continue to give warm fuzzies to the rest of your students in the days to come. Encourage each child to wear his warm fuzzy for the entire day as a reminder that he's a lovable critter, too!

Here's a warm fuzzy from me to you!

Complimentary Comments

Take a moment during your closing circle time to send youngsters home feeling good about their accomplishments. Instead of packing away the day's projects in backpacks or cubbies, gather them in a pile for your closing circle time. Call a child forward, show his project to the class, and make one positive observation about his work for all to hear. For instance say, "Edward, I can tell you took extra time with your painting today. You should feel proud of yourself!" Continue to give each child a courteous comment about his work—compliments of the teacher.

Behind My Name

You name it—this activity's got it! Help youngsters learn to appreciate their names and also learn some history behind their names. In advance ask parents to help their youngsters practice reciting their first, middle, and last names. Also request from each family a note explaining why their child's name was selected. At the library, check out a book that tells the origin and meaning of names. Then make certificates that tell the meaning of each student's name.

Ask a few children each day to state their first, middle, and last names. Then read their parents' notes and present each youngster with her name certificate. Pride is the name of this game!

listened at storytime

David

held door for Kristen

shared blocks with Kyle

My name is:
Tia
It is Greek.
It means princess.

You're Shining

Watch your shining stars beam with confidence as you recognize individual achievement. In advance write each child's name on a separate large star cut from yellow construction paper. As a class, brainstorm ideas about how students can shine like stars at school. Solicit responses such as sharing, listening to directions, or playing cooperatively. Explain that you will be watching for star behavior and accomplishments over the next several days. As you notice positive behavior, record your observations on the construction-paper stars. At the end of each day, proclaim one or two children's star behavior; then pin their stars on their clothing for all to see.

SNOW

It's "Snow" Secret!

Invite your youngsters to have some frosty fun using their senses. To prepare, put fresh snow or crushed ice in a resealable plastic bag. Place the plastic bag in a brown paper bag and fold down the top. Have your youngsters form a circle; then hold up the bag for the class to see. Challenge the class to guess what is in the bag by using their senses. As you pass the bag around the circle, ask each child to grasp the top of the bag and describe how heavy it feels. Next invite the students to shake the bag and describe how it sounds. Then open the top of the bag and encourage your little ones to smell the contents without peeking. Bring a chilly end to this guessing game by inviting youngsters to reach inside and feel the cold snow. If desired, follow up with a treat for the eyes and taste buds—snow cones!

There's 'snow-body' like me!

"Snowbody" Like Me!

Youngsters will feel special when they discover that, just like snowflakes, no two children are alike. To prepare, fold and snip several coffee filters to make unique snowflake shapes. Glue each snowflake to a black construction-paper background, and display it for all to see. Explain to the class that scientists have never discovered two snowflakes that are alike. Then tell youngsters that they have something in common with snowflakes. Have each youngster turn to face another child. Invite the partners to look at each other and discuss physical characteristics, such as eye, hair, and skin color. Help each child conclude, "There's 'snowbody' just like me!"

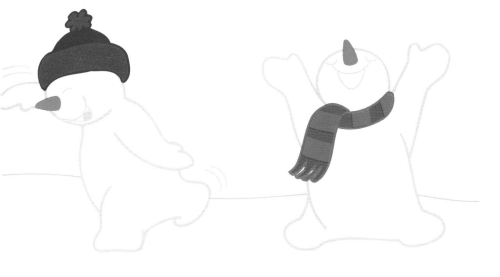

Silly Snowmen

Give a lesson in listening as your youngsters size up these snowmen. In advance, cut from white polyester batting one small, one medium, and one large circle. Ask a student volunteer to place the circles randomly on your flannelboard as you call out each circle's size—small, medium, or large. Next ask the child to arrange the circles to form a snowman. If necessary, clarify concepts such as *bottom, top,* or *above.* Next have another volunteer follow your directions to arrange the circles differently on the flannelboard. As each subsequent volunteer creates an arrangement, invite youngsters to shout out the result—"Snowman!" or "No-man!"

I'm Melting!

Put stronger subtraction skills at your students' fingertips with this snowy song. Count down with repeated verses until the sun has melted every flake.

(sung to the tune of "Five Little Ducks")

[Five] snowflakes come out to play,
Down from the sky so far away.
Sunshine comes out strong and bright.

One little flake melts out of sight.

(Hold up [five] fingers.)
(Wiggle fingers downward.)
(Wave other hand over five fingers.)
(Put one finger down.)

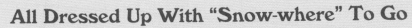

All Dressed Up With "Snow-where" To Go

There's "snow" substitute for warm clothing on a snowy day. Sing the following song during circle time as your little ones act out bundling up in each article of clothing.

(sung to the tune of "The Farmer In The Dell")

It's cold outside today.
It's cold outside today.
Brrr! Brrr! It's cold outside!
Let's get dressed to play.

I put my snowsuit on.
I put my snowsuit on.
Brrr! Brrr! It's cold outside!
I put my snowsuit on.

Continue with other verses:

I put my snow boots on…
I put my mittens on…
I put my wool hat on…
I put my warm scarf on…

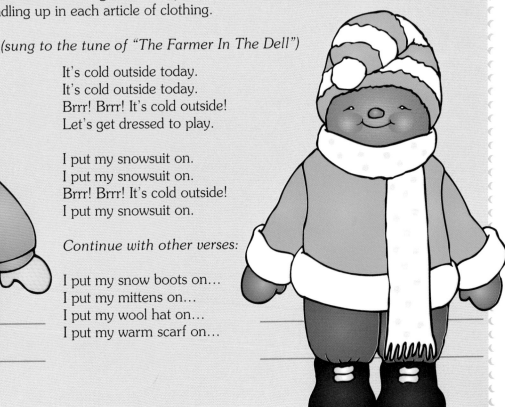

Space

Circle-Time Countdown

Give your future astronauts some practice with counting backward. Explain to the children that when a spaceship is ready to be launched, the people at mission control count backward as they confirm that everything is working properly. Use your fingers to demonstrate how to count down from ten; then have students echo you and copy your finger movements. After the children have had plenty of practice counting backward, display numeral flash cards with numerals from 1 to 10. Ask a volunteer to identify the numeral on a designated card; then have him lead the class in the countdown. For example, if the numeral on the card is 6, have the children stand and count, "6-5-4-3-2-1—Blast off!" Encourage youngsters to jump high each time they complete their countdown.

A Twinkling Tune

Give your little space travelers a review of our solar system with this twinkling tune. Encourage the children to create additional verses of their own.

A Solar System Song
(sung to the tune of "He's Got The Whole World In His Hands")

We've got [the solar system] in our sights.
We've got [the solar system] in our sights.
We've got [the solar system] in our sights.
We've got [the solar system] in our sights.

We've got the golden Sun…

We've got the twinkling stars…

We've got Pluto and Mars…

Space Exploration

Have your little astronauts suit up for a simulated space flight to the moon. Encourage students to use their imaginations as you lead them in the following dramatization. First pretend to put on space suits. Enter the spaceship and fasten seat belts. Push the lever to start the engines. Count down, "10-9-8-7-6-5-4-3-2-1—Blast off!" As you enter outer space, steer the spaceship to the left, to the right, and then straight ahead. Turn quickly to miss a meteor. As you approach the moon, release the landing gear and gently land. Unbuckle seat belts and exit the spacecraft. Take big, slow steps around the moon. Gather some space rocks; then prepare for your safe return home.

ABC Space

Reinforce the alphabet with this exploration of space vocabulary. To prepare, write the alphabet in a left-hand column of a sheet of chart paper. Then read several books to the class about astronauts and the solar system. Encourage the children to think of space-related words that represent each letter of the alphabet, such as *astronaut, blastoff,* and *constellation.* If desired, accept more than one response for each letter. Add to the list daily as your unit continues. Once the list is complete, encourage each youngster to illustrate one or more words from the list. Label each drawing and highlight the letter of the alphabet it represents. Put the drawings in alphabetical order, and add a cover with the title "ABC Space." Reviews of this class book will be sky-high!

Astronaut Adventure

Launch into circle time with these astronaut antics.

Astronaut, astronaut, turn around.
Astronaut, astronaut, touch the ground.
Astronaut, astronaut, leap so high.
Astronaut, astronaut, reach the sky.
Astronaut, astronaut, fly around Mars.
Astronaut, astronaut, touch the stars.
Astronaut, astronaut, walk on the Moon.
Astronaut, astronaut, come home soon.

Turn around.
Touch the ground.
Jump.
Stand on toes with arms reaching up.
Pretend to fly with arms to sides.
Open/close hands like twinkling stars.
Take big, slow steps.
Sit down, pretzel-style.

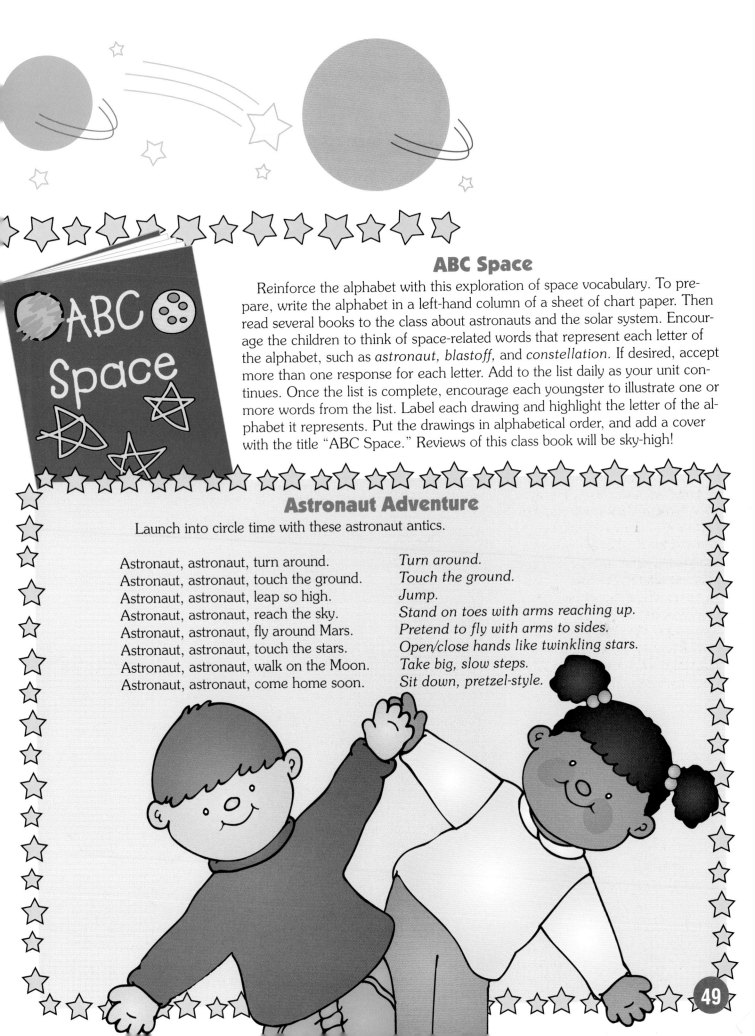

Spiders And Bats

Blind As A Bat

"Bat-tle" the misconception that bats are blind. In fact, all species of bats can see almost as well as humans. Explain to your children that bats rely on their senses of sight and smell to help them find food at night. Then challenge your little ones to find food as bats do. Darken the room and set out a tray of fragrant snacks, such as fresh orange slices or peanut-butter crackers. Place the tray at a distance from your students. Can your youngsters see or trace the smell of food in the semidarkness? Once the children have identified where and what the food is, invite them to relax and snack like bats!

Spider Diet

Help your little ones learn about a spider's diet with this silly song that will have a web spinning and children grinning! To begin, discuss with youngsters the types of foods that spiders like to eat, such as grasshoppers, bees, and ants. Then ask them to pretend that they are spiders, spinning a web to catch a tasty meal. What would *they* like to catch for lunch? Begin the web spinning by passing a ball of yarn around a circle of seated youngsters. Have each child hold on to the free section of the yarn with one hand and pass the ball with the other hand. Sing the song below, inviting the child holding the ball of yarn at the end of the verse to name a sensible or silly spider food. Continue spinning the web until everyone has had a turn to name a spider food.

I'm A Hungry Spider
(sung to the tune of "The Itsy Bitsy Spider")

I am a hungry spider, ready for my lunch.
I'll spin a web and catch something to munch!
I'll catch a beetle or a bumblebee.
But what would you catch in your web if you were me?

Leggy Spiders

Get a leg up on your spider unit with this guessing game. In advance gather four pictures—one each of a person, a four-legged animal, an insect, and a spider. Put the pictures in a basket. Show the pictures to the class and discuss the number of legs each creature possesses. Then invite your youngsters to play this guessing game. Ask a student to select a picture from the basket. Say the following chant; then ask the student to count aloud the number of legs belonging to her secret creature. Challenge the other children to determine (from the number of legs) whether the secret creature is man or beast, insect or spider.

2 - 4 - 6 - 8,
Counting legs is really great!
8 - 6 - 4 - 2,
Creature, how many legs have
     you?

Batty Colors

Little ones will go batty over this colorful fingerplay! In advance prepare a set of five bat finger puppets for each child by cutting two-inch squares from black, brown, gray, red, and yellow construction paper. Stamp each square with a bat stamp; then tape each square into a cylinder shape sized to fit on a child's fingertip. (Be certain the bat is showing.) Have each child put her finger puppets on one hand. Then sing the following song. As each color of bat is mentioned, have youngsters show their corresponding bat puppets.

Where Is Blue Bat?
(sung to the tune of "Where Is Thumbkin?")

Where is [blue] bat, where is [blue] bat?
Here I am, here I am.
How are you this morning?
Very well, I thank you.
Fly away, fly away.

Where is brown bat…
Where is gray bat…
Where is red bat…
Where is yellow bat…

Hang In There

Teach your little ones about a bat's nighttime flights and daytime sights with this song.

I'm A Little Bat
(sung to the tune of "I'm A Little Teapot")

I'm a little bat. I fly at night,

Searching for food that tastes just right.
When the morning comes, I settle down
And sleep all day turned upside down.

*Hands held outstretched
     with thumbs crossed.
Wave fingers as if flying.
Slowly stop waving fingers.
Turn hands upside down.*

Thanksgiving

Gobblin' Good

Practice counting as your little turkeys sing this gobblin' good tune. Have youngsters display the corresponding number of fingers while counting forward and backward. For added fun, select ten children to act out the song. Signal each of the ten little turkeys to stand in turn as you sing the first stanza and sit in turn during the second stanza.

Gobble, Gobble
(sung to the tune of "Ten Little Indians")

1, 2, 3, a-gobblin',
4, 5, 6, a-gobblin',
7, 8, 9, a-gobblin',
10 little turkeys gobblin'.

10, 9, 8, a-gobblin',
7, 6, 5, a-gobblin',
4, 3, 2, a-gobblin',
1 little turkey gobblin'.

A Pilgrim's Perspective

As your little ones discuss life as it was during the first Thanksgiving, encourage them to act out the lines and create new verses for this song.

Let's Rock At Plymouth!
(sung to the tune of "We Wish You A Merry Christmas")

The Pilgrims were busy catching fish.
The Pilgrims were busy catching fish.
The Pilgrims were busy catching fish.
Oh, what a day's work!

The Pilgrims were busy planting corn…
The Pilgrims were busy finding berries…
The Pilgrims were busy hunting deer…

The Word Bird

Strengthen vocabulary as your youngsters add a plumage of Thanksgiving words to this featherless fowl. To prepare, cut a feather for each child and one large featherless turkey from construction paper. (Or draw a turkey on your chalkboard.) Each day during the month of November, solicit from a student volunteer a Thanksgiving-related word, such as *turkey, Pilgrims,* or *cranberries.* On a single feather, make a simple drawing to illustrate the word, and label it in large print. Then tape the feather to the turkey. As each new feather is added, have the class review all the previous Thanksgiving words. Challenge older children to read the words as you point to them in random order. For added fun, encourage the children to copy and illustrate the words into a class book about Thanksgiving.

A Basket Of Blessings

Your students are certain to learn how much they have to be grateful for as they pass a basket of blessings. Explain to your youngsters that during the Pilgrims' first winter in their new land, they did not have enough food. But by Thanksgiving they were thankful to eat the corn and other crops that they had grown. Then give each child a single kernel of unpopped corn. Pass a small basket around the circle. Have each child name one food for which he is thankful as he puts his kernel in the basket. In the following days, have children put more kernels in the basket as they name other things for which they are grateful concerning school, nature, and their families.

Terrific Turkey Talkin'

Reinforce ordinal numbers with this fingerplay about some frightened fine-feathered friends.

Five little turkeys behind a stack of hay,	
The first one said, "I really hate this day!"	*Put hands over eyes.*
The second one said, "There's a farmer over there!"	*Put hands on hips.*
The third one said, "We don't have a prayer!"	*Point in one direction.*
The fourth one said, "This isn't any fun!"	*Put hands together as if praying.*
The fifth one said, "Let's run and run and run!"	*Make a sad face.*
So they all took a deep breath,	*Pretend to run.*
And off like a shot,	*Take a deep breath.*
The five little turkeys escaped from the pot!	*Make zooming motion with hand.*
	Cheer.

After your little ones have memorized the fingerplay, assign five student volunteers to each play the role of one of the turkeys. Signal each turkey to recite his line; then have the rest of the class say the remaining lines with you.

Transportation

Sounds Abound In Traffic

"Choo-choo-choose" this rhyme to teach your youngsters about vehicles and the sounds they make. Display a picture of a train, an airplane, a boat, and a car; then ask the children to make the sound of each vehicle. Next say the following rhyme, pausing to allow the children to give the suggested sound for each line. Provide visual clues by holding up the picture that corresponds to each line.

> I hear [choo-choo-choo] when a train chugs by.
> I hear [zoom, zoom, zoom] when a plane flies high.
> I hear [toot, toot, toot] when a boat glides past.
> I hear [beep, beep, beep] when a car drives fast.

"Bus-tling" Along

Rev up your youngsters' language and math skills with this activity that explores positional words and ordinal numbers. In advance set up rows of chairs to resemble the seats on a bus. Then gather youngsters and explain that they'll be going on an imaginary bus ride. Have students line up for the bus; then use positional words as you arrange the line. For example, say, "Joe, stand *in front of* Karla. Louis, stand *behind* her. Mary Lou, be *next* after Ashley." Then give directions for the youngsters to climb aboard the pretend bus, and use positional words and ordinal numbers as you direct students where to sit: "Ellen, sit in the *second* row. Darnell, sit in the *fourth* row. Katie, sit *beside* Darnell." Ask little ones where they'd like to go; then pretend to drive them to their destination. Repeat the activity for the bus ride home.

Follow up with a small-group activity, having students follow your directions to seat toy people in a toy bus.

"Car-tegories"

Get some mileage out of this game that categorizes vehicles. In advance request that parents send their child to school with one of his favorite toy vehicles. (Have extras on hand for children who may need them.) Invite youngsters to sit in a circle with their vehicles parked on the floor in front of them. Then begin the game by asking children with vehicles of a designated color to stand and show their toys. Once you've covered all the colors, name a different attribute by which the vehicles could be sorted, such as number of wheels or doors, size, or mode of travel. Your youngsters will find that detailing their vehicles can be fun!

Favorite Set Of Wheels

Keep your transportation unit going in high gear with this fun song about every child's favorite set of wheels.

Shiny Brand-New Trike
(sung to the tune of "Little Red Caboose")

Shiny brand-new trike,
Shiny brand-new trike,
Shiny brand-new trike—I love to ride.

Wind blows through my hair,
Ride it everywhere.
Shiny brand-new trike—I love to ride!

Traveling To School

Enthusiasm will be riding high as you sing this transportation song 'round the classroom. Ask your youngsters if they travel to school by walking with an adult, riding in a car, or riding on a bus (or van). Then sing the following song together, and invite each youngster to stand during the verse that describes how she travels to school.

We'll Be Coming To Our School
*(sung to the tune of
"She'll Be Coming 'Round The Mountain")*

We'll be traveling to our school in different ways.
We'll be traveling to our school in different ways.
We'll be traveling to our school, we'll be
    traveling to our school,
We'll be traveling to our school in different ways.

We'll be riding to our school in our cars….
We'll be riding to our school on the bus….
We'll be walking to our school hand in hand….

Valentine's Day

Be My Valentine!

Mystery Valentine

Have your youngsters send "love-ly" sentiments one another's way with this valentine game. Set a chair at a distance from the children. Invite one child to sit in the chair with his back to the class. Silently signal another child to stand directly behind—but out of the sight of—the child in the chair. Have her disguise her voice and say, "Be my valentine." Then have her sit back down. Watch for giggles and grins as the child in the chair tries to identify his secret admirer. After the secret has been revealed, have the two players exchange places; then select another child to send a hearty greeting.

A Heartfelt Song

This color-review song will have your little songbirds singing with all their hearts. Purchase a bag of large candy conversation hearts. Identify the color of each heart as you give one to each child. Then sing the following song repeated times, substituting the various colors of the candy hearts.

(sung to the tune of "Where Is Thumbkin?")

Teacher: Where is [pink] heart?
          Where is [pink] heart?
Students: Here I am!   *Children with pink hearts stand and sing.*
          Here I am!
All: Happy Val-en-tine's day!
          Happy Val-en-tine's day!
Teacher: Eat your heart.   *Children eat hearts.*
          Now sit down.   *Children sit down.*

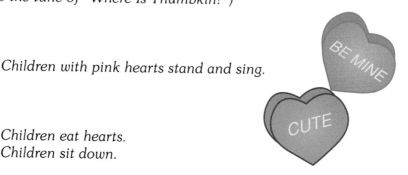

Special Delivery

Make distributing valentines carefree instead of chaotic with this tip. In advance tape a school photo (or other close-up photo) of each child to a sheet of copy paper. Duplicate a copy of the resulting class gallery for each child. To each copy, attach a note to parents requesting that they assist their children in cutting out the pictures and pasting them to the fronts of their valentine envelopes.

During your valentine celebration, invite a few children at a time to distribute their valentines, using the photos on their envelopes to guide them as they make their special deliveries.

Valentine History

Share some valentine history with your little sweethearts. Long ago, ladies' names were written on pretty slips of paper and placed in a glass jar. Gentlemen would come forward and draw a name from the jar. The lady whose name was drawn became his valentine. Another valentine custom was that a gentleman would wear his valentine's name on his sleeve for several days. (The saying "wearing his heart on his sleeve" probably came from this tradition.)

Try this modified version of these bygone customs. Write your children's names on construction-paper hearts and place them in a large jar. Invite one child at a time to select a name from the jar; then use masking tape to attach the name to his sleeve. Next give him a candy heart to present to his chosen valentine. Encourage your young gentlemen and ladies to be kind and thoughtful to their sweetheart friends for the remainder of the day.

Broken Hearts

Mend broken hearts while strengthening number sense with this matching activity. Cut enough large heart shapes from construction paper for half your class. Program one side of each heart with a numeral and the other side with a corresponding set of hearts. Then cut each paper heart up the middle between the numeral and its corresponding set of hearts. Put the broken hearts in a box and mix them up.

Have the class form a circle; then distribute one half of a heart to each child. Ask the class to hold up their broken hearts for all to see. Challenge each youngster to find the missing half of his heart. Once a child has found a classmate with his heart's missing half, invite the pair to stand side by side and mend the broken heart. In the following days, reinforce other basic skills in a heartbeat by programming a new set of hearts with rhyming pictures or upper- and lowercase letters.

ZOO HABITATS

Here's a tune about animal habitats that really hits home. To prepare, gather pictures of various animals that live in the water and on land. Label the top of a piece of chart paper with the headings "Water" and "Land." Add a small drawing of waves and a sketch of grass and a tree to cue nonreaders.

Show youngsters the animal pictures and discuss where each animal lives. As you sing the following song, hold up each animal picture. Then solicit your students' help in taping the animal picture under the corresponding habitat.

OH WHERE, OH WHERE?
(sung to the tune of "Oh Where, Oh Where Has My Little Dog Gone?")

Oh where, oh where does a
[dolphin] live?
Oh where, oh where is his home?
Does he live in water or on the land?
Oh where, oh where does he roam?

water   land

FEEDING TIME

Ready for feeding-time frenzy at the zoo? Talk about the different kinds of foods zoo animals eat; then sing this song. If desired, follow up with a related reading of *Sam Who Never Forgets* by Eve Rice (Greenwillow Books).

(sung to the tune of "Ten Little Indians")

One little, two little, three little fishies,
Four little, five little, six little fishies,
Seven little, eight little, nine little fishies,
To feed the hungry seals.

One pail, two pails, three pails of oats,
Four pails, five pails, six pails of oats,
Seven pails, eight pails, nine pails of oats,
To feed the hungry zebras.

One ripe, two ripe, three ripe bananas,
Four ripe, five ripe, six ripe bananas,
Seven ripe, eight ripe, nine ripe bananas,
To feed the hungry monkeys.

ANONYMOUS ANIMALS

Take your students on an imaginary walk through the zoo! Ask your little ones to pretend that they have just arrived at the zoo. Ask them to close their eyes and try to picture what it looks like. Verbally walk them through the main gate as you describe the sounds, smells, and sights. At the first animal exhibit, give the children a series of clues to help them guess the identity of the animal. For example your clues might include: "This animal has four legs. It has orange and black stripes." When your students have arrived at a guess, encourage them to make the sound of the mystery animal (for example a loud tiger roar). Continue your walk through the zoo, describing more animals that you meet along the way.

ZOO GROUPS

This sorting activity is in a category all its own. Use the animal pictures gathered for "Zoo Habitats" (page 58). Give each child a picture; then call out a feature that some of the animals possess, such as stripes, spots, or tails. If a child is holding an animal that fits the description, have him stand and show his picture. Solicit other attributes by which the animals might be sorted, such as size, number of legs, or habitat.

COUNTING CRITTERS

Count your way through the zoo with this fingerplay adaptation of *Brown Bear, Brown Bear, What Do You See?* by Bill Martin, Jr. (Henry Holt And Company, Inc.).

One bear, one bear, who's with you?	*Wiggle pointer finger.*
Two funny monkeys in the zoo.	*Wiggle two fingers.*
Monkeys, monkeys, who's with you?	
Three striped zebras in the zoo.	*Wiggle three fingers.*
Zebras, zebras, who's with you?	
Four king lions in the zoo.	*Wiggle four fingers.*
Lions, lions, who's with you?	
Five huge elephants in the zoo.	*Wiggle five fingers.*
Elephants, elephants, who's with you?	
Visiting children—just like you!	*Wiggle fingers on both hands.*

Weather Pictures
Use with "Weather Watchers" on page 12.

Leaf Pictures
Use with "Leaves In Action" on page 32 and "Problems With Leaves" on page 33.

©1998 The Education Center, Inc. • *Busy Kids*™: *Circle Time* • TEC538

Use with "Directional Dinos" on page 14 and "Dinosaur, Dinosaur" and "A Daily Dose Of Dinosaur Math" on page 15.

©1998 The Education Center, Inc. • *Busy Kids™: Circle Time* • TEC538

Vegetable Patterns

Use with "Mystery Veggie," and "Farmer In The Garden" on page 28 and "Read All About It!" on page 29.

©1998 The Education Center, Inc. • Busy Kids™: Circle Time • TEC538

Use with "Tune In To Food," and "Food Clues" on page 38 and "Pyramid Match" on page 39.

cracker

popcorn

Wheaty Cereal

cereal

pretzels

bagel

cookie

carrot

celery

orange

apple

cheese

Vanilla Yogurt

yogurt

peanuts

chicken

CHOCOLATE BAR

candy bar

french fries

ABOUT THE AUTHORS

dayle timmons has been teaching "at-risk" preschoolers for eight years at the highly acclaimed Alimacani Elementary School, a national model school in Jacksonville, Florida. During her 25-year career in teaching special education, dayle has been named teacher-of-the-year in three different school districts. dayle enjoys sharing her ideas with other teachers and is a regular contributor to *The* Preschool *Mailbox®*. dayle lives in Jacksonville, Florida, with her husband, Jim, and two children. ▶

◀ **Jan Brennan** taught young children in a public school setting for seven years before deciding to home-school her own children, preschool through fourth grade. Jan contributes to *The* Preschool *Mailbox®* on a regular basis, currently by writing the feature "Building Bridges." Jan lives in Avon, Connecticut, with her husband, three sons, and a preschool-age daughter.

Lisa Leonardi has eight years of experience teaching full-day kindergarten and first grade. She is currently president of the Norfolk Cooperative Preschool and enjoys giving workshops and seminars for parents. Lisa has been sharing her ideas with teachers for three years as a freelance writer for The Education Center, Inc. Lisa lives in Norfolk, Massachusetts, with her husband and two daughters. ▶

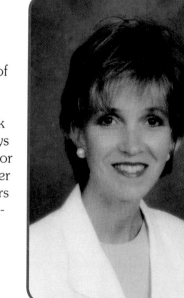

◀ **Ann Flagg** has been working with young children in both public and private settings for 11 years. Ann taught preschool for five years and recently served as the director of Clarion Christian Preschool in Clarion, Pennsylvania. Writing for The Education Center, Inc., has been an ongoing part of Ann's contribution to the education of young children. Ann lives in Mesa, Arizona, with her husband and daughter.